YOUR KNOWLEDGE HAS VALUE

Bibliographic information published by the German National Library:

The German National Library lists this publication in the National Bibliography; detailed bibliographic data are available on the Internet at http://dnb.dnb.de .

Imprint:

Copyright © 2007 GRIN Verlag, Open Publishing GmbH
Print and binding: Books on Demand GmbH, Norderstedt Germany
ISBN: 9783668258341

This book at GRIN:

http://www.grin.com/en/e-book/133404/the-pronounciation-of-german-loanwords-in-english-an-analysis-of-phonological

Stefanie Dietzel

The Pronounciation of German Loanwords in English. An Analysis of Phonological Differences

GRIN Publishing

GRIN - Your knowledge has value

Since its foundation in 1998, GRIN has specialized in publishing academic texts by students, college teachers and other academics as e-book and printed book. The website www.grin.com is an ideal platform for presenting term papers, final papers, scientific essays, dissertations and specialist books.

Visit us on the internet:

http://www.grin.com/

http://www.facebook.com/grincom

http://www.twitter.com/grin_com

Philipps Universität Marburg

Institut für Anglistik und Amerikanistik

HS Contrastive Linguistics

Summer Term 2007

The Phonology of German
Loanwords in English

by

Stefanie Dietzel

Table of Contents

1 Introduction

"English does not have many German loanwords – at least not many of common use – but those it does have are a rather more mixed bunch than such stereotypic lists might imply." (Stubbs 1998:19) With his statement, Stubbs refers to those linguists who claim that the small number of German loanwords in English only originate from specific historical contexts. In his paper, he wants to revise this belief and show that also more general terms are adapted from German to English. My paper will focus on the pronunciation of the most frequent German borrowings in English, which derive from different contexts. It will point out the influence of English phonology on the realization of these loanwords by native speakers of English. First, I will emphasise the main differences between English and German phonology. A short overview of historical incidents will illustrate the impact of German on the English vocabulary. A definition describes what is meant by the term loanwords and a classification will distinguish between different types of loanwords. In order to get presentable information about the most frequently occurring loanwords, I collected my data from different corpora and I checked the phonetic realization using two pronunciation dictionaries, namely the *Longman Pronunciation Dictionary* and the *English Pronunciation Dictionary* by Wells and Jones. Additionally, I taped three native speakers of British English for my investigation. I will provide the list of borrowings, which represents my data collection via the two online corpora *Oxford English Dictionary (OED)* and the *British National Corpus (BNC)*. The list will concentrate on the latest loanwords occurring in English since 1800. The study of the etymology is useful in order to show that these words are direct loans from German. According to the comparison of German and English phonological particularities, and using the list as a basis, I will formulate a hypothesis about the changes in the pronunciation. After that, my paper will show the results of the recording of the three native speakers. Simultaneously, the words will be analysed with respect to their phonetic realization. Finally, I will sum up the main results and conclude whether the hypothesis is relevant.

2 Contrastive Phonology of German and English

In order to be able to analyse the phonology of German loanwords in English, it is necessary to give an overview of the main phonological differences between English and German. Therefore, this paragraph will show the corresponding consonant and vowel inventories and point out where they vary. My research is based on the vowel and consonant system of

Received Pronunciation, which represents the most prestigious, generally accepted accent of British English.

2.1 Consonants

Contrasting the consonant inventories of English and German																	
English									**German**								
Plosives	p	b	t	d			k	g		p	b	t	d			k	G	
Fricatives	f	v	θ	ð					h	f	v					x		h
			s	z	ʃ	ʒ						s	z	ʃ	ʒ			
Affricates					tʃ	dʒ				pf		ts				ks		
Nasals	m		n							m		n						
Liquids & semi-vowels	w		l	r		j						l	r	j				

(Kortmann 2005:182)

Regarding the table of consonants above, and given the fact that some consonants from the German system are missing in the English one and vice versa, we expect that native speakers of English will have difficulties in pronouncing certain German loanwords, which contain consonants that are not available in the English inventory. At least, the result will not sound like the original German word.

For example, English lacks the fricatives /ç/ and /x/, in German also known as the *ich-Laut* and *ach-Laut*. It is debatable whether the affricates /pf/, /ts/ and /ks/ should be regarded as one phoneme each or as two separate phonemes. Most linguists agree that these affricates exist in the German but not in the English consonant inventory.

Besides the complete absence of certain consonants, there are also consonants which occur in both languages, but their phonemic realization differs between English and German. This phenomenon indicates that both languages use different allophones. For example, the pronunciation of /r/ in British English is post-alveolar, whereas in German it is uvular. Moreover, German uses a clear /l/ in every position, while English makes a distinction between clear [l] and dark [ɫ]. The usage of final devoicing, i.e. the voiceless articulation of obstruents like /b/, /d/ and /g/ at the end of a syllable, is a typical German phenomenon and does not occur in English (Kortmann 1998:181-182).

Another typical feature of German is the phenomenon that vocalic onsets are often preceded by a glottal stop /ʔ/ (Cannon 1994:114).

2.2 Monophthongs

English monophthongs: German monophthongs :

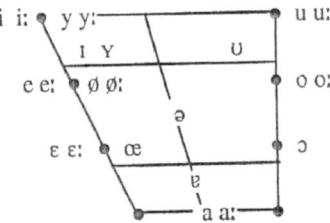

(English monophthongs: https://en.wikipedia.org/wiki/File:RP_Cardinal_Vowels.JPG)

(German   monophthongs   based   on: http://www.linguistik-online.de/26_06/attaviriyanupap.html)

The most striking difference between the English and the German vowel system is that English lacks all rounded front vowels like /y:/ and /ø/. English does not use /e:/, /ɛ:/ and /o:/, either. The monophthongs /æ/, /ʌ/, /ɒ/ and /ɜ:/, which can be found in English, are not present in German (Kortmann 1998:182-183).

2.3 Diphthongs

English diphthongs:

second component	close front	close back	central
Close front			Iə
mid-open front	eI		ɛə
mid-central		əʊ	
Open	aI	aʊ	
back and rounded	ɔI		ʊə

(http://www.germanistik.unibe.ch/attaviriyanupap/FoliePhonetik.3.pdf,   accessed   10 November 2007)

German diphthongs:

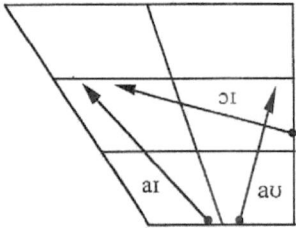

(http://www.linguistik-online.de/26_06/attaviriyanupap.html)

In contrast to English, which has eight diphthongs, the German vowel system contains only three, namely /ai/, /ɔi/ and /aʊ/ (Kortmann 1998:183).

3 German Loanwords in English

3.1 Definition of Loanwords

A loanword is an expression, which is directly adapted from one language to another language. Loanwords can also be referred to as "borrowings" [INT2].

The implementation of loans from foreign languages into the English vocabulary is a natural phenomenon. A language is always dynamic, i.e. changes are normal and the development of the vocabulary continues constantly. It is always influenced by words from other languages (Stubbs 1998:21).

When two languages get in contact, it is very likely that words are borrowed by one language from the other. Adopting the linguistic features typical of one language is easier within two languages, which belong to the same language group, as it is the case with English and German. The larger the typological distance between two languages, the more difficult is the transfer of linguistic items. But English and German are both West Germanic languages and the forms are partly similar.

English has borrowed some German words which are lexically more similar to the original than phonetically. Thus the graphemes resemble each other more than the phonetic realizations. That is because new phonemes are rarely adopted by a language. Therefore the question arouses how German loanwords are pronounced in English. (Cannon 1994:113-114)

6

3.2   The Context and History of German Loanwords in English

Most loanwords are adopted by a language due to significant historical or cultural events. Others have a specific scientific background. Some English words, which originate from German, are known from the time of the Second World War (e.g.: *Nazi*, *Third Reich*, and *Führer*). A predominant type of borrowings is specific vocabulary from mineralogy, chemistry, biology and further fields of natural sciences. Technical terms like *chromosome*, *Hertz*, or *quartz* are examples of German loanwords from the field of natural sciences. International scientific papers contain German expressions like *adduct*, *emulsoid*, and *mutase*, which again derive from Greek and Latin origins. Further words such as *dirndl* and *lederhosen* represent German cultural stereotypes. Moreover, the corpus of loanwords contains proper names of famous persons or locations such as *Hitler*, *Leipniz*, or *Rheingold*. There is not a large amount of borrowings from German in English and most words are not known by the majority of speakers of English, but a small number can be found in common use (Stubbs 1998:19-21).

3.3   Classification of Loanwords

The semantic development of the borrowings differs from word to word. While some expressions exclusively refer to the original meaning from the period of World War 2 (e.g. *panzer*), others occur in a more general context:

(1) a. there is to be a blitz on incorrect grammar

b. a blitzkrieg of media type

(Stubbs 1998:20)

There are also pure semantic loans, namely borrowings of the meaning of a word, which is transferred to an existing English form, like the sense of *Kurfürst* to *elector* (Cannon 1994:22). The word *unconscious* also illustrates this phenomenon: Its meaning refers to the German philosopher Freud since his publications from the 1920s (Stubbs 1998:24). Some direct loans maintain both their sense as well as their form (e.g.: *Abgesang*), but others are changed in their form (e.g.: *Afrikanerdom*) (Cannon 1994:22).

Besides direct loans, further types of borrowings include loan translations, indirect loans, and pure German words in English. The first type describes cases in which mainly compounds are directly translated from German into English and the meaning

7

is maintained (e.g.: *Antikörper – anti-body, Machtpolitik – power politics, Regenwald – rain forest*). Indirect loans are words with a more complex background. They derive originally from German but passed a development through Yiddish or American English into British English. Examples are *bagel* and *schmalz*. Rarely, pure German words occur in special cases, for example because there is no appropriate English translation, or because the context is about specific German events (*hochgeboren* and *Künstlerroman*).

Although German loanwords in English occur very rarely in every-day-English, there are many items especially in English academic areas which originate from German. For example, technical terms in the field of linguistics include a variety of German borrowings such as *ablaut, loan word, High German*, or *umlaut* (Stubbs 1998:21-24).

4 Methodology, Data Collection and Hypothesis

This paper will not focus on specific items from a scientific context but on the pronunciation of the most frequent terms which occur in a more general context in every-day language or in newspaper articles. Also, it concentrates on the direct loans from German. It will analyse words which maintained their original meaning in the course of time and which have not significantly changed in their form.

Stubbs gives a number of loanwords which are useful for my investigation. In order to back up the relevance of his list, I re-examined the frequency of these and further words by using the BNC and the OED corpora. In addition, I concentrated on those words, which are indicated as borrowings from German in the pronunciation dictionaries. Besides that, I included those items which were known by the three test persons. For this purpose I also used German loanwords which I found in an English newspaper, for example *Führer* and *Leitmotiv*. After the selection of 37 borrowings, my test persons were asked to articulate the words. I then compared the accurate English pronunciation of the particular words according to the pronunciation dictionaries with the original pronunciation, as specified in the German dictionary *Duden*.

4.1 The Most Frequent Borrowings

The following table lists the most frequently occurring German loanwords in English during the last 200 years, their orthographic appearance in both languages, and a comparison of the German and the English pronunciation. The main differences are restricted to pronunciation. The form remains the same in most cases. The only striking feature is that the first letters of nouns are usually transformed from a capital to a small letter, which is typical of English spelling. The reason why exceptions like *Fahrenheit* and *Neanderthal* begin with a capital letter is probably because these words derive from names.

Loanword	Pronunciation in BE	Original German Word	German Pronunciation
angst	æŋkst	Angst	Aŋst
Autobahn	'ɔ:təʊbɑ:n	Autobahn	'aʊtoba:n
blitz	blɪts	Blitz	blɪts
blitzkrieg	'blɪtskri:g	Blitzkrieg	'blɪtskri:k
bratwurst	'brætwɜ:st	Bratwurst	'bra:tvʊrst
dachshund	'dæksənd	Dachshund	'dakshʊnt
delicatessen	delɪkə'tesən	Delikatesse	delika'tɛsə
edelweiss	'eɪdəlwaɪs	Edelweiß	'e:dlvais
ersatz	'eəzæts	Ersatz	ɛɐ'zats
Fahrenheit	'færənhaɪt	Fahrenheit	'fa:rənhait
festschrift	'festʃrɪft	Festschrift	'fɛstʃrɪft
frankfurter	'frænkfɜ:tə	Frankfurter	'frankfʊrtɐ
frau	fraʊ	Frau	frau
Fuhrer/Fuehrer	'fjʊərə	Führer	'fy:rɐ
Gesellschaft	gə'zelʃɑ:ft	Gesellschaft	gə'zɛlʃaft
Gestapo	ge'sta:pəʊ	Gestapo	ge'sta:po
hamburger	'hæmbɜ:gə	Hamburger	'hambʊrgɐ
herr	heə	Herr	hɛr
hertz	hɜ:ts	Hertz	hɛrts
hinterland	hɪntəlænd	Hinterland	'hɪntɐlant
kaiser	'kaɪzə	Kaiser	'kaizɐ
kindergarten	'kɪndəgɑ:tən	Kindergarten	'kɪndɐgartn
kitsch	kɪtʃ	Kitsch	kɪtʃ
krieg		Krieg	
lederhosen	'leɪdəhəʊzən	Lederhosen	
leitmotiv	'laitməʊti:f	Leitmotiv	'laitmoti:f
nazi	'nɑ:tsi	Nazi	'nɑ:tsi
Neanderthal	ni'ændətɑ:l	Neanderthal	ne'andɐta:l
pretzel	'pretsəl	Brezel	
Reich	raɪk	Reich	raiç
rucksack	'rʌksæk	Rucksack	'rʊkzak

sauerkraut	'saʊəkraʊt	Sauerkraut	'zaʊɐkraut
strudel	'stru:dəl	Strudel	'ʃtru:dl
wanderlust	'wɒndəlʌst	Wanderlust	'vandɐlʊst
wiener	'wi:nə	Wiener	'vi:nɐ
wurst		Wurst	vʊrst
zeitgeist	'zaɪtgaɪst	Zeitgeist	'tsaitgaist

4.2 Hypothesis

Cannon and Pfeffer (1994), claim that the native speakers of a language usually stick to the phonological rules of their mother tongue. For example, native speakers of German would use the glottal stop /ʔ/ and the velar fricative /x/ in English, whereas English native speakers would replace those phonemes, which are not used in their language, with an English similar sound. This would be the case in *Achtung* or in *Bach*. Here, the German /x/ would be replaced with the phoneme /k/, which is also velar. Where speakers of German would use final devoicing, as in the word ending –s, speakers of English would rather pronounce the ending as a voiced /z/ instead of a voiceless /s/ (Cannon 1994:114). Thus, we can make the following assumptions:

a) The pronunciation of German loanwords in English is generally influenced by the phonology of the speaker's mother tongue and does not sound like the original in most cases.

b) In case there are no equivalent phonemes available in the English inventory, we can expect the speaker to replace the lacking phoneme by another similar segment from the English inventory.

c) As languages are dynamic and there are different accents of English, it is likely that several native speakers of the same language will pronounce the same loanword differently.

d) The phonetic realization by the three different test persons will presumably be slightly different from the standardized versions denoted in the pronunciation dictionaries, because the speakers do not use perfect Received Pronunciation, and they know only a small number of the words mentioned above.

Contrasting the consonant and vowel inventories of English and German, I suppose that the differences may lead to difficulties for speakers of English, when they pronounce German loanwords. My research, in which I taped native speakers of British

English, will show the accuracy of this hypothesis and point out the differences in phonetic realization.

5 Analysis of Phonological Differences

5.1 Results of Audio Recording

The pronunciation of the German loanwords by the three English women matches the transcriptions of the dictionaries in most cases. Nevertheless, small differences can be recognized. These variations may be due to the speakers' individual linguistic knowledge, their awareness of history, and their cultural background. The three young women are between 24 and 27 years old and they grew up in Southern England. Although their parents come from Africa or Asia, their mother tongue is English.

For my research, I provided them with a list of German loanwords in English. They had to pronounce each word on the list without knowing the original pronunciation. The fluency of their utterances would suggest that some words are more familiar to the test persons and some less. Expressions like *Wirtschaftswunder* or *Thüringer sausage*, which were indicated as German borrowings by Pfeffer (1987), were pronounced hesitantly by all speakers, which can be an evidence for their low frequency in every-day-English. Therefore, I did not pay attention to those words in my research.

5.2 Analysis

The phonological differences that emerge from the influence of the English phonological inventory can be classified into the three types of changes within a word, namely the substitution of consonants, monophthongs and diphthongs.

5.2.1 Consonantal differences

The list of loanwords contains various items which illustrate the substitution of certain consonants. But there is a difference between substitutions without an equivalent English phoneme, and thus a replacement is required, and those, where the change is due to orthographic reasons. The former case can be illustrated by the following example:

Final devoicing of German loanwords in English occurs although in German it is unusual.

11

(1)   a. German: *Blitzkrieg* /blɪtskriːk/ versus English: *blitzkrieg* /blɪtskriːg/

b. German: *Dachshund* /dakshʊnt/ versus English: *dachshund* /dæksənd/

c. German: *Hinterland* /hɪntɐlant/ versus English: *hinterland* /hɪntəlænd/

The first example (1)a. shows that the voiceless velar plosive at the end of the syllable is replaced with its voiced equivalent. The voiceless alveolar plosives in the loanwords in (1)b. and (1)c. are also exchanged by voiced ones, which are produced at the same place and with the same manner of articulation.

A further phenomenon is the use of different allophones. The words below are examples of different realizations of the same phoneme /r/.

(2)   a. German: *Blitzkrieg* /blɪtskriːk/ versus English: *blitzkrieg* /blɪtskriːg/

b. German: *Bratwurst* /braːtvʊrst/ versus English: *bratwurst* /brætwɜːst/

c. German: *Fahrenheit* /faːrənhait/ versus English: *fahrenheit* /færənhaɪt/

The phonemic realization of /r/ in British English is post-alveolar, whereas in the original German version it is uvular.

As mentioned above, English lacks the phoneme /ç/. Therefore, native speakers of English are likely to produce a different phoneme instead.

(3)   a. German: *Reich* /raiç/ versus English: *Reich* /raik/

In this example, the fricative /ç/ is replaced with the plosive /k/, because /k/ is part of the English consonant inventory and it is phonetically similar to /ç/; both are voiceless and velar.

Furthermore, the onset combination of /ʃtr/ is not common in English.

(4)   a. German: *Strudel* /ʃtruːdl/ versus English: *strudel* /struːdəl/

In addition, native speakers of English tend to substitute an item of a loanword although the German phoneme is part of their consonant system. The explanation for this is that speakers of English refer to the graphemes for the articulation of words. For example, they pronounce the letter <w> as /w/ in contrast to Germans, who use the voiceless labiodental fricative /v/:

(5)   a. German: *Bratwurst* /braːtvʊrst/ versus English: *bratwurst* /brætwɜːst/

b. German: *Edelweiß* /eːdlvais/ versus English: *edelweiss* /eɪdəlwaɪs/

c. German: *Wanderlust* /vandɐlʊst/ versus English: *wanderlust* /wɒndəlʌst/

12

Furthermore, the letter <s> in loanwords is often uttered as a voiceless /s/ in front of vowels at the beginning of a syllable instead of the voiced /z/:

(6)   a. German: *Rucksack* /rʊkzak/ versus: English: *rucksack* /rʌksæk/

      b. German: *Sauerkraut* /zaʊɐkraut/ versus English: *sauerkraut* /saʊəkraʊt/

Test person two pronounces the word *lederhosen* like /leɪdəhɔsən/.

Other examples show that this phenomenon is not a general principle, but that <s> in that position can remain a voiced /z/:

      c. German: *Ersatz* /ɛɐ'zats/ versus English: *ersatz* /eəzæts/

      d. German: *Gesellschaft* /gə'zɛlʃaft/ versus English: *Gesellschaft* /gə'zelʃɑːft/

Test persons one and three say /'leːdəhəʊzən/ and /'lidəhəʊzən/ when they pronounce the word *lederhosen*.

German has no dental fricatives. Therefore, the letter combination <th> is pronounced like the alveolar plosive /t/, while English people would normally use the dental fricatives /θ/ or /ð/. Although the version of the loanword *Neanderthal* in the English dictionaries is transcribed as /ni'ændətɑːl/, test persons two and three pronounce the word like /ni'ændəθɑːl/.

Another striking feature is that English lacks the affricate /ts/ as in *zeitgeist*. Native speakers of English would realize the pronunciation as /'zaɪtgaɪst/, whereas the German equivalent would be /'tsaitgaist / in its original version. Here, the affricate /ts/ is replaced with the voiced alveolar fricative. This is due to orthographic reasons. The letter <z> is usually articulated as /z/ in English. Nevertheless, in the case of the word *hertz*, which is a technical term, the combination of the letters <ts> is pronounced correctly, according to the German word Hertz: German / hɛrts / versus English /hɜːts/. This example illustrates that speakers of English have the ability to utter the affricate /ts/ and that they use it only if the letter combination denotes this directly according to English orthographic rules.

5.2.2 Differences among Monophthongs

Changes in the realization of vowels occur even more often than changes of consonants.

The letter <a> is often realized as /æ/ in English, while it is pronounced as /a/ in German.

(1)   a. German: *Angst* /aŋst/ versus English: *angst* /æŋkst/

      b. German: *Bratwurst* /'bra:tvʊrst / versus English: *bratwurst* /'brætwɜ:st/

      c. German: *Fahrenheit* /'fa:rənhait/ versus English: *Fahrenheit* /'færənhaɪt/

      d. German: *Hamburger* /'hambʊrgɐ/ versus English: *hamburger* /'hæmbɜ:gə/

The English vowel inventory lacks all rounded front vowels. Therefore, /y:/ is replaced with the combination of the phonemes /jʊ/ as illustrated below:

(2)   a. German: *Führer* /'fy:rɐ/ versus English: *führer* /'fjʊərə/

This example points out that the rounded front vowel /y:/ cannot be uttered by native speakers of English, unless they learn German. Instead, by inserting the liquid /j/ before the alternative vowel /ʊ/, the speakers of English try to make the loanword sound similar to the German original. My findings show that the pronunciation of loanwords largely depends on the speaker's historical knowledge because the term *führer* has its origins in German history. While the first and the second test persons simply replaced the vowel /y:/ with the phonemes /ʊ/ or /ɜ/, the third test person used the combination /iə/, which shows that she has heard of the term before and tried to imitate the German pronunciation.

On the contrary, other items with historical background are not familiar to either of the three test persons. They do not know the term *krieg*, but this is still an interesting example. The letter combination of <ie> indicates a long /i:/ in German. In contrast to that, it is not a common grouping of vowels in English. Test person one uses the correct German pronunciation, while test person two replaces /i:/ by /eɪ/ and test person three changes it into /iə/. Within the word *wiener*, which is indicated as /'wi:nə/ in the English dictionaries, test person two substitutes the phoneme /i:/ by /aɪ/.

Some long vowels from the German inventory are not present in the English vowel system, either. That is why speakers of English refer to a substitution of the phoneme /e:/:

(3)   a. German: *Edelweiß* /'e:dlvais/ versus English: *edelweiss* /'eɪdəlwaɪs /.

Besides that, the phoneme /ɛ/ cannot be found in English. This can be demonstrated by the following cases:

(4)   a. German: *Hertz* / hɛrts/ versus English: *hertz* / hɜ:ts /

      b. German: *Festschrift* /'fɛstʃrɪft/ versus English: *festschrift* /'festʃrɪft/

14

Additionally, the phoneme /o/ is normally substituted because it does not exist in English:

(5)   a. German: *Autobahn* /'aʊtobaːn/ versus English: *autobahn* /'ɔːtəʊbɑːn /

   b. German: *Leitmotif* /'laitmotiːf/ versus English: *leitmotiv* /'laitməʊtiːf /

Another inconsistency between the English dictionaries and the test persons can be due to different varieties of English. Not all native speakers pronounce all words equally. There are social, cultural and regional differences which play a role and affect the individual's pronunciation. This might be an explanation for the use of the phoneme /ʌ/, where others would use /æ/. In the case of the word *Neanderthal*, the dictionaries suggest the following pronunciation: /ni'ændətɑːl/. However, test persons one and two use /a/ in the second syllable. The reason might be that they have a strong British accent.

5.2.3 Differences among Diphthongs

The substitutions which occur among diphthongs are due to orthographic reasons. As English has more diphthongs than German, native speakers of English do not have difficulties in uttering the three German diphthongs /ai/, /ɔi/ and /aʊ/. These are also present in the English inventory. Several examples show that there are no such difficulties:

(1)   a. German: *Edelweiß* /eːdlvais/ versus English: *edelweiss* /eɪdəlwaɪs/

   b. German: *Kaiser* /'kaizɐ/ versus English: *kaiser* /'kaɪzə/

   c. German: *Sauerkraut* /'zaʊɐkraut/ versus English: *sauerkraut* /'saʊəkraʊt/

On the contrary, there are cases in which speakers of English do not maintain the diphthong but replace it:

   d. German: *Autobahn* /'aʊtobaːn/ versus English: *autobahn* /'ɔːtəʊbɑːn /

In this case the dictionary suggests the substitution of /aʊ/ by /ɔː/.

It is remarkable that test person three pronounces the word *Reich* as indicated in the dictionaries, namely as /raɪk/, while the other two realize the letters <ei> as /iː/. They do not use a diphthong here because they have not heard the expression before. The orthographic combination of <ei> is normally not pronounced as /aɪ/, but those who

15

realize the diphthong according to the German pronunciation are probably aware of the fact that *Reich* originates from German. In most contexts it refers to the German Reich.

6   Conclusion

Although the number of German loanwords in English is restricted, some items play a significant role in every-day-language because in some cases there are no suitable English equivalents which could replace the loanwords.

According to the analysis, we can state that the hypothesis is to some extend verified with regard to the four assumptions made before. To begin with, the list of the most frequent German loanwords in English compared the English pronunciation with the German one. The research has shown that speakers are influenced by the phonological inventories of their mother tongue and that the pronunciation of the German borrowings is determined by English phonological aspects. Secondly, speakers of English tend to substitute those phonemes, which are not present in their consonant and vowel systems, by phonetically similar ones if possible. Moreover, the comparison of the three test persons underlines that each individual has his own way of pronouncing unknown or hardly known loanwords. The more unfamiliar the term, the more likely are the single pronunciations by different speakers dissimilar. The investigation has also shown that the phonetic realization of borrowings by the test persons does not always correspond to the standardized versions denoted in the pronunciation dictionaries. We can notice small differences in the use of phonemes.

An additional question that arises is whether native speakers of English would tend to adapt to the original German pronunciation when they learn German as a foreign language.

The progress in communication technology and the intensification of international cooperation leads to the assumption that the exchange of words between countries like Germany and England or other English-speaking areas will continue in the future. Thus, the corpus of German borrowings in English will grow, while very old terms are likely to disappear from the English vocabulary.

A continuous topic worth a discussion would be the pronunciation of English loanwords in German and the difficulties of native speakers of German when they pronounce English borrowings.

7 References

Kortmann. 2005. *English Linguistics: Essentials.* Berlin: Cornelsen Verlag. pp. 181-183.

Pfeffer / Cannon. 1994. *German Loanwords in English – An Historical Dictionary.* Cambridge: University Press. pg. 22, pp. 113-114.

Pfeffer. 1987. *Deutsches Sprachgut im Wortschatz der Amerikaner und Engländer: vergleichendes Lexikon mit analytischer Einführung und historischem Überblick.* Tübingen: Niemeyer. pp...

Stubbs. 1998. "German Loanwords and Cultural Stereotypes." In *English Today.* Cambridge: University Press. pp.19-26.

http://dictionary.oed.com, accessed 8 November 2007.

http://www.natcorp.ox.ac.uk, accessed 8 November 2007

English Pronunciation Dictionary, Longman Pronunciation Dictionary

YOUR KNOWLEDGE HAS VALUE

- We will publish your bachelor's and master's thesis, essays and papers

- Your own eBook and book - sold worldwide in all relevant shops

- Earn money with each sale

Upload your text at www.GRIN.com
and publish for free